HOW TO DRAW FOR KIDS

A Simple Step-by-Step Drawing Book

This book belongs to :

....

TIPS TO USE THIS BOOK

Gather a sharp pencil and a good eraser for a smooth drawing experience. You might also want to use colored pencils to add some color to your drawings.

Sit on a chair with a straight back and at a suitable height for drawing. Make sure you are comfortable to maintain good posture while drawing.

Each drawing is broken down into simple steps. Start your drawing with light lines. This makes it easier to fix mistakes and keep your sketch clean. Using light lines also helps with smoother transitions and adjustments as you improve your drawing.

Use the blank spaces to practice and improve your skills. You can also color your finished drawings any way you like to make them unique and personal.

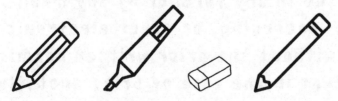

WHAT'S INSIDE

+ Activity Pages for Curious Kids

Alligator

Alligators have very big mouths with lots of sharp teeth – about 80 teeth in total!

START

Practice Here

Ants can carry objects 50 times their own body weight

ANIMALS

Ant

Ants can carry objects 50 times
their own body weight

START

Practice Here

ANIMALS

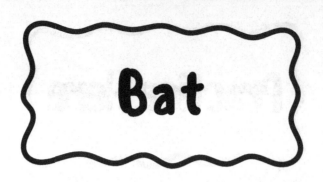

Bat

Bats are the only mammals that can truly fly

Practice Here

Bears have strong paws with long claws that help them dig for food and climb trees!

ANIMALS

Bear

Bears have strong paws with long claws that help them dig for food and climb trees

Practice Here

ANIMALS

Bee

Bees make a buzzing sound with their
wings that flap really fast

START

Practice Here

ANIMALS

Butterfly

Butterflies start their lives as caterpillars
and transform inside a chrysalis

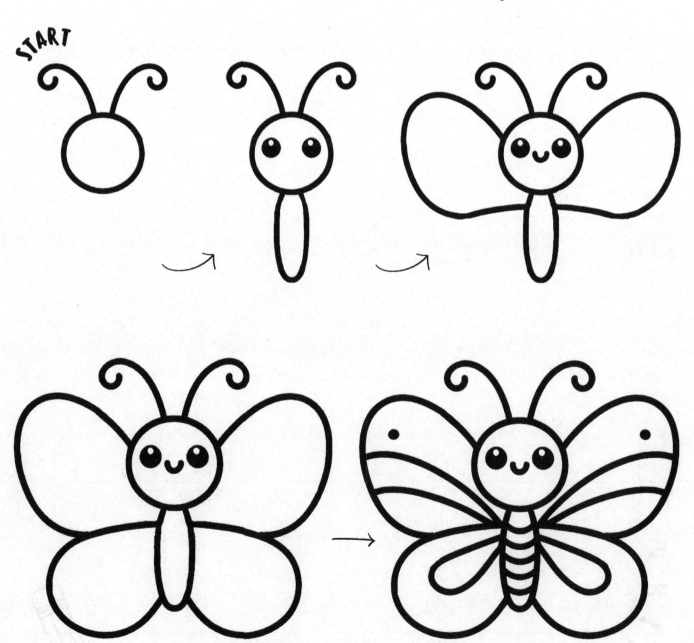

START

Practice Here

ANIMALS

Camel

Camels can go for weeks without water,
storing fat in their humps

START

Practice Here

ANIMALS

Cat

Cats spend around 70% of their lives sleeping

START

ANIMALS

Chicken

Chickens can remember over 100 different faces of people or animals

START

Practice Here

ANIMALS

Cow

Cows are surprisingly good swimmers and enjoy taking a dip in the water

ANIMALS

Crab

Crabs walk sideways because their legs are built to move in that direction

START

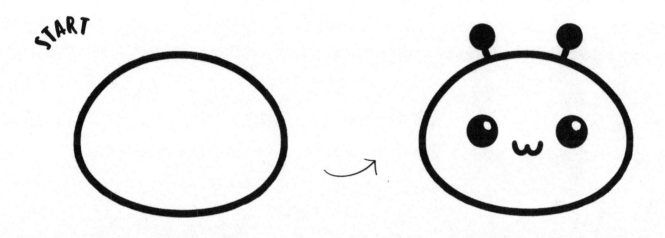

Practice Here

ANIMALS

Deer

Deer have a great sense of hearing and can move their ears in all directions to listen for danger

START

Practice Here

ANIMALS

Dinosaur

Dinosaurs lived millions of years ago, and some were as small as chickens!

Practice Here

Dogs have an amazing sense of smell,
about 40 times better than humans!

ANIMALS

Dog

Dogs have an amazing sense of smell,
about 40 times better than humans!

START

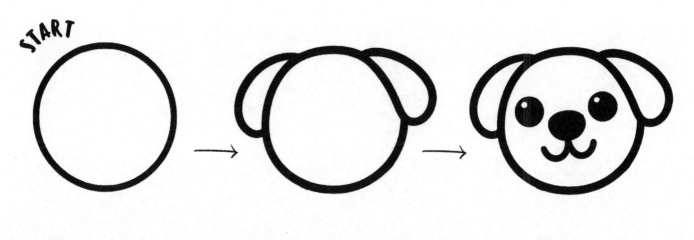

Practice Here

ANIMALS

Dolphin

Dolphins are very smart and love to play; they can even recognize themselves in mirrors

START

Practice Here

ANIMALS

Dragonfly

Dragonflies can fly in any direction, even backwards!

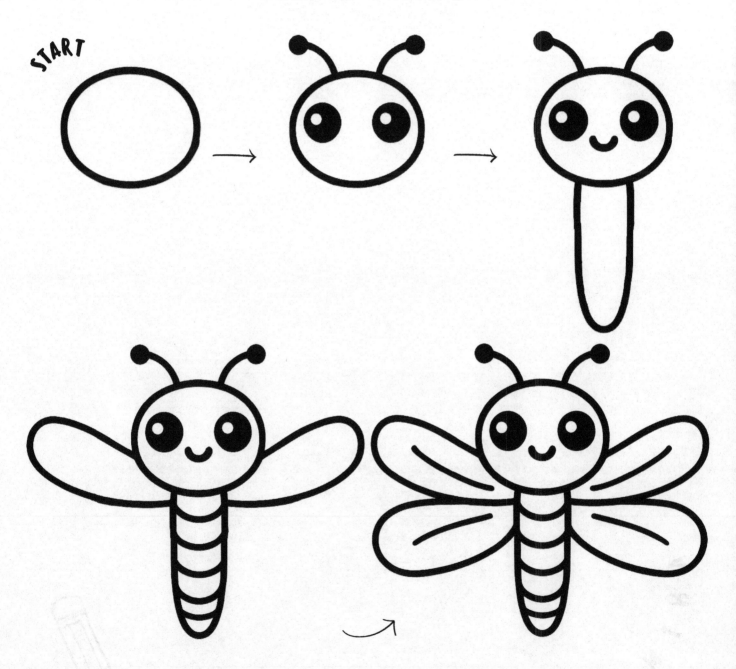

Practice Here

ANIMALS

Duck

Ducks have waterproof feathers to keep them dry while swimming

Practice Here

Eagles have excellent eyesight and can spot their prey from a mile away.

ANIMALS

Eagle

Eagles have excellent eyesight and can spot their prey from a mile away

START

Practice Here

ANIMALS

Elephant

Elephants are the largest land animals and can use their trunks to drink water

START

Practice Here

Fish

Fish use their gills to breathe
underwater

START

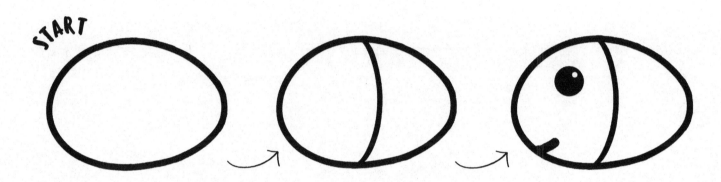

Practice Here

A
N
I
M
A
L
S

Flamingo

Flamingos live in large colonies that can include thousands of birds

START

Practice Here

ANIMALS

Fox

Foxes are great night hunters and have excellent vision

Practice Here

ANIMALS

Frog

Frogs absorb water through their skin
so they don't need to drink

Practice Here

ANIMALS

Giraffe

Giraffes have long necks to help them
reach leaves high up in trees

Practice Here

ANIMALS

Goose

Geese can live up to 20 years in the wild

START

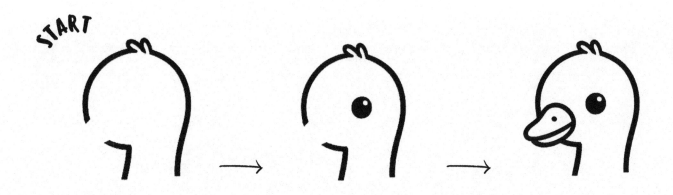

Practice Here

ANIMALS

Hedgehog

Hedgehogs roll into a ball and use their spines to protect themselves from predators

START

Practice Here

Hippos can hold their breath for about five minutes underwater.

ANIMALS

Hippo

Hippos can hold their breath for about
five minutes underwater

Practice Here

ANIMALS

Horse

Horses can sleep both lying
down and standing up

START

ANIMALS

Jellyfish

Jellyfish don't have brains,
hearts, or bones

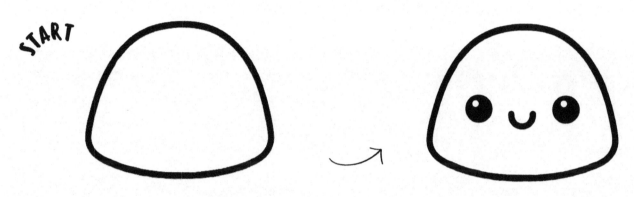

START

Practice Here

Kangaroos have very strong back legs
that help them jump high and far

ANIMALS

Kangaroo

Kangaroos have very strong back legs
that help them jump high and far

Practice Here

Koala Bear

Koalas sleep up to 18 hours a day and only eat eucalyptus leaves

START

Practice Here

ANIMALS

Ladybug

Not all ladybugs are red – they can be
yellow, orange, and even black

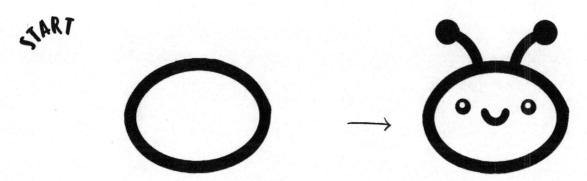

Practice Here

Lions can run up to 50 miles per hour,
but only for short distances.

ANIMALS

Lion

Lions can run up to 50 miles per hour,
but only for short distances

Practice Here

ANIMALS

Lizard

Lizards love to bask in the sun to warm
up because they are cold-blooded

START

Practice Here

Llamas are very social animals and
like to be with other llamas.

ANIMALS

Llama

Llamas are very social animals and like to be with other llamas

START

ANIMALS

Monkey

Monkeys use their tails to help them balance and swing in trees

START

Practice Here

Owl can rotate their head almost all the way around to see behind them

ANIMALS

Owl

Owls can rotate their heads almost all the way around to see behind them

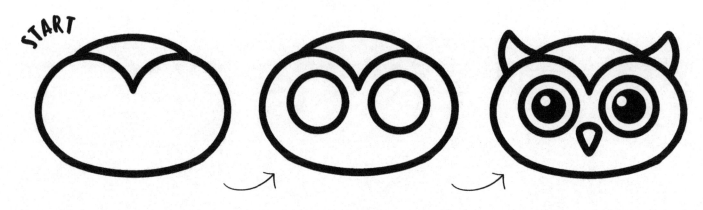

START

Practice Here

A
N
I
M
A
L
S

Panda

Pandas spend most of their day
eating bamboo

START

Practice Here

Pig

Pigs are very smart and can
learn tricks just like dogs

START

Practice Here

Rabbits have big ears that help them hear predators from far away.

ANIMALS

Rabbit

Rabbits have big ears that help them
hear predators from far away

Practice Here

ANIMALS

Raccoon

Raccoons have hands that are a lot like human hands, which help them grab and open things

START

Practice Here

ANIMALS

Shark

Sharks have lots of teeth, and if one falls out,
a new one grows right back in its place

START

Practice Here

ANIMALS

Sheep

Sheep can jump pretty high –
some can even clear a 4-foot fence

START

Practice Here

ANIMALS

Snail

Some snails can sleep for several years
if the weather is too dry

START

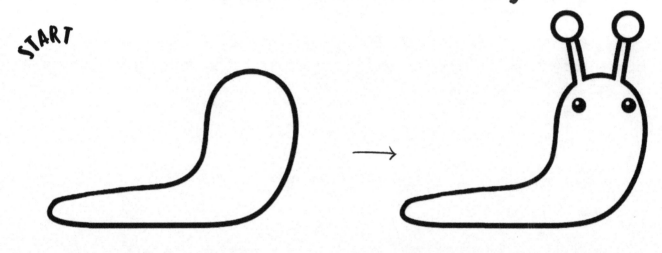

Practice Here

ANIMALS

Spider

Spiders have eight legs, which makes them great climbers and fast runners

Practice Here

ANIMALS

Starfish

If a starfish loses an arm, it can grow
a new one – just like magic!

START

Practice Here

A tiger's roar can be heard
up to 2 miles away

ANIMALS

Tiger

A tiger's roar can be heard
up to 2 miles away

START

Practice Here

A N I M A L S

Turkey

Turkeys sleep in trees at night to stay
safe from predators

START

Practice Here

ANIMALS

Matching Words Puzzle

Match or pair the words from the following list.

_____ 1. Rabbit	A. Mud
_____ 2. Sheep	B. Pond
_____ 3. Chicken	C. Cave
_____ 4. Elephant	D. Milk
_____ 5. Monkey	E. Bone
_____ 6. Dog	F. Honey
_____ 7. Cow	G. Grass
_____ 8. Bee	H. Banana
_____ 9. Whale	I. Web
_____ 10. Squirrel	J. Ocean
_____ 11. Pig	K. Hump
_____ 12. Deer	L. Egg
_____ 13. Goat	M. Stripes
_____ 14. Turtle	N. Trunk
_____ 15. Zebra	O. Claws
_____ 16. Duck	P. Carrot
_____ 17. Spider	Q. Antlers
_____ 18. Camel	R. Wool
_____ 19. Crab	S. Shell
_____ 20. Bat	T. Nut

Animals Crossword

Solve the following puzzle based on the clues given!

Across

[2] An animal with a mask on its face and a ringed tail

[6] A bird that makes holes in trees with its beak

[9] A small animal covered in spines that curls into a ball

[10] An animal with long legs and antlers on its head

Down

[1] A red animal with a long, bushy tail and pointy ears

[3] A little animal with stripes that stores food in its cheeks

[4] A small animal with a bushy tail that loves to eat nuts

[5] A big, furry animal that sleeps all winter

[7] A bird with big eyes that says "hoot" at night

[8] An animal with a big, flat tail that builds homes in water

Animals Word Scramble

Unscramble the following list of shuffled words to meaningful words!

GAAONROK

ADNAP

ALEPEHNT

GUEINPN

ZLGIYZR EARB

IEGRFFA

AAOKL

LRPOA ARBE

CALAPA

OMOKOD ANOGRD

ILON

BLAD EGEAL

UME

ERD FXO

NSOW DELOPRA

Farm Animals Word Search Puzzle

Solve the following puzzle by finding all the hidden words!

```
P H O R S E K T A E
I B P D U C K U A H
G D O N K E Y R C M
G B S C A L F K H R
L O G O A T A E I A
L C O W C L P Y C B
A E H S T A C G K B
M B E E M O A E I
A S N Y E B C U N T
T O O M S S H E E P
```

Words List

Cow	Turkey	Sheep	Donkey
Pig	Goose	Goat	Llama
Chicken	Hen	Horse	Lamb
Duck	Calf	Rabbit	Bee

Jungle Animals Word Search Puzzle

Solve the following puzzle by finding all the hidden words!

```
P U M A S N A K E G
A A R T M N I O E O
L L I O N G P L R I
S E P G N R U J E I
L O A E K I A A P L
O P R R E E N G H L
T A R T Y I A U A A
H R O T O U C A N L
P D T B O A R R T A
P A N T H E R N I O
```

Words List

Lion	Monkey	Jaguar	Toucan	Puma
Tiger	Parrot	Gorilla	Panther	Iguana
Elephant	Leopard	Snake	Sloth	Boa

Birds Word Search Puzzle

Solve the following puzzle by finding all the hidden words!

```
B P F O R S W A N P
L A L W H O B D I S
U R A O B A B L D P
E R M P C I W I S A
B O I E E M A K N R
I T N E A N O W L R
R W G R N G G D R O
D A O G B I L U A W
R C A N A R Y E I A
K S L B D U C K Y N
```

Words List

Sparrow	Owl	Duck	Canary
Robin	Eagle	Parrot	Swan
Bluebird	Penguin	Flamingo	Hawk

Find Missing Vowels

Find the missing letters in the following list of words!

L ( ) ( ) N — Big cat with a majestic mane.

T ( ) G ( ) R — Striped big cat from Asia.

( ) L ( ) P H ( ) N T — Large mammal with a trunk.

K ( ) N G ( ) R ( ) ( ) — Australian marsupial with a pouch.

P ( ) N D ( ) — Black and white bear from China.

P ( ) ( ) C ( ) C K — Bird with colorful tail feathers.

G ( ) R ( ) F F ( ) — Tallest animal with a long neck.

D ( ) L P H ( ) N — Smart sea mammal that can jump.

( ) W L — Nocturnal bird with big eyes.

P ( ) R R ( ) T — Colorful bird that can mimic speech.

P ( ) N G ( ) ( ) N — Flightless bird that waddles.

R ( ) B B ( ) T — Small mammal with long ears.

B ( ) ( ) R — Large mammal that hibernates.

F L ( ) M ( ) N G ( ) — Pink bird that stands on one leg.

F ( ) X — Cunning animal with a bushy tail.

MAZE

Solution

Match or pair the words from the following list.

P	1. Rabbit	A. Mud
R	2. Sheep	B. Pond
L	3. Chicken	C. Cave
N	4. Elephant	D. Milk
H	5. Monkey	E. Bone
E	6. Dog	F. Honey
D	7. Cow	G. Grass
F	8. Bee	H. Banana
J	9. Whale	I. Web
T	10. Squirrel	J. Ocean
A	11. Pig	K. Hump
Q	12. Deer	L. Egg
G	13. Goat	M. Stripes
S	14. Turtle	N. Trunk
M	15. Zebra	O. Claws
B	16. Duck	P. Carrot
I	17. Spider	Q. Antlers
K	18. Camel	R. Wool
O	19. Crab	S. Shell
C	20. Bat	T. Nut

Solution

Solve the following puzzle based on the clues given!

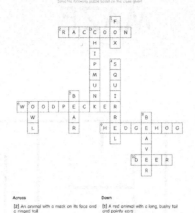

Across

[2] An animal with a mask on its face and a ringed tail

[6] A bird that makes holes in trees with its beak

[4] A small animal covered in spines that curls into a ball

[10] An animal with long legs and antlers on its head

Down

[1] A red animal with a long, bushy tail and pointy ears

[3] A little animal with stripes that stores food in its cheeks

[4] A small animal with a bushy tail that loves to eat nuts

[5] A big, furry animal that sleeps all winter

[7] A bird with big eyes that says "hoof" at night

[8] An animal with a big, flat tail that builds homes in water

Solution

Unscramble the following list of shuffled words to meaningful words!

GAAONROK	KANGAROO
ADNAP	PANDA
ALEPEHNT	ELEPHANT
GUEINPN	PENGUIN
ZLGIYZR EARB	GRIZZLY BEAR
IEGRFFA	GIRAFFE
AAOKL	KOALA
LRPOA ARBE	POLAR BEAR
CALAPA	ALPACA
OMOKOD ANOGRD	KOMODO DRAGON
ILON	LION
BLAD EGEAL	BALD EAGLE
UME	EMU
ERD FXO	RED FOX
NSOW DELOPRA	SNOW LEOPARD

Solution

Solve the following puzzle by finding all the hidden words!

Words List

Cow	Turkey	Sheep	Donkey
Pig	Goose	Goat	Llama
Chicken	Hen	Horse	Lamb
Duck	Calf	Rabbit	Bee

Solution

Solve the following puzzle by finding all the hidden words!

Words List

Lion	Monkey	Jaguar	Toucan	Puma
Tiger	Parrot	Gorilla	Panther	Iguana
Elephant	Leopard	Snake	Sloth	Boa

Solution

Solve the following puzzle by finding all the hidden words!

Words List

Sparrow	Owl	Duck	Canary
Robin	Eagle	Parrot	Swan
Bluebird	Penguin	Flamingo	Hawk

Solution

Find the missing letters in the following list of words!

- L I O N — Big cat with a majestic mane.
- T I G E R — Striped big cat from Asia.
- E L E P H A N T — Large mammal with a trunk.
- K A N G A R O O — Australian marsupial with a pouch.
- P A N D A — Black and white bear from China.
- P E A C O C K — Bird with colorful tail feathers.
- G I R A F F E — Tallest animal with a long neck.
- D O L P H I N — Smart sea mammal that can jump.
- O W L — Nocturnal bird with big eyes.
- P A R R O T — Colorful bird that can mimic speech.
- P E N G U I N — Flightless bird that waddles.
- R A B B I T — Small mammal with long ears.
- B E A R — Large mammal that hibernates.
- F L A M I N G O — Pink bird that stands on one leg.
- F O X — Cunning animal with a bushy tail.

Made in the USA
Columbia, SC
13 December 2024

49201250R00063